DYNAMIC

FLEXIBILITY

Alan Pearson

A & C Black • London

Metric to Imperial conversions

1 centimetre (cm)	=	0.394 in
1 metre (m)	=	1.094 yd
1 kilometre (km)	=	1093.6 yd
1 kilogram (kg)	=	2.205 lb

First published 2004
by A&C Black Publishers Ltd
37 Soho Square, London W1D 3QZ
www.acblack.com

Copyright © 2004 by SAQ International Ltd

ISBN 0 7136 6452 5

A CIP catalogue record for this book is available from the British Library.

A&C Black uses paper produced with elemental chlorine-free pulp, harvested from managed sustainable forests.

Acknowledgements
Cover photograph courtesy of Image State; all other photographs courtesy of Alan Pearson; illustrations courtesy of Steve Gilbert.

Typeset in Photina
Printed and bound in Great Britain by Bell & Bain Ltd, Thornliebank, Scotland

Speed, Agility & Quickness International Limited Trade mark numbers:

'SAQ' ® Britain and Northern Ireland No. 2156613
'SAQ' ® European Community No. 001026277
'SAQ Speed, Agility, Quickness' ® Australia

SAQ ™

SAQ Programmes™
SAQ Equipment™
SAQ Training™
SAQ Accreditation Awards™

In addition to the above, the following trademarks are in current commercial use by SAQ International and have been for several years in respect to their products and services:

Fast Foot™ Ladder
Viper Belt™
SAQ Continuum™
Jelly Balls™
Micro Hurdles™
Macro Hurdles™
Speed Resistor™
Sprint Sled™
Power Harness™
Sonic Chute™
Agility Disc™
Side Strike®
Flexi-cord™
Velocity Builder™
Heel Lifter™
Visual Acuity Ring™
Peripheral Vision Stick™
Break Away Belt™ and Tri-Break Away Belt™
Dynamic Flex®
Bunt Bat™

The SAQ Continuum, SAQ Training, SAQ Programmes, SAQ Accreditation Awards and SAQ Equipment are products and services of Speed, Agility & Quickness International Limited (SAQ INTERNATIONAL) and its licensees. Only individual or corporate holders of valid SAQ Trainer certificates or valid SAQ Training licenses issued by SAQ INTERNATIONAL may offer products or services under the SAQ brand name or logo (subject to terms).

Discover more about SAQ Programmes, SAQ Accreditation Awards and SAQ Equipment online at www.saqinternational.com

Contents

Forewords

Dynamic Flex is the way we should warm up because when we play sport and exercise it is dynamic. Warming up for physical activity must therefore be dynamic. Dynamic Flex warms up the cardiovascular and neuromuscular systems and can be adapted to the needs of all sports and activities with ease. This new book is clear, informative and simple to follow and I recommend it to anyone involved in sport or physical activity, whatever their age or ability, professional or amateur.

Peter Friar BSc (Hons), MSc, MScP, SRP
Head Physiotherapist and Sport Scientist at Sunderland F.C.

Dyamic flexibility is optimally achieved with the Dynamic Flex Warm-Up. Dynamic Flex adapts to the individual movement needs of children and encourages them to extend their skills naturally. It fits in with their behaviour and natural development. It is easy to follow, making it ideal for parents and anyone working with children and young people, providing a structured learning opportunity and allowing children to obtain and improve essential movement skills.

Dr Madeleine Portwood
Specialist Senior Educational Psychologist
Chairperson of the Education Commitee of the
Dyspraxia Foundation

Acknowledgements

Thank you to Sarah, David, Marc, Angus and Silvana for their great support, to Rebecca for her administration of the project and a very special thank you to Steve Gilbert for his superb illustrations.

Have you ever watched a cat move from rest to play? Its movements are instantly and instinctively dynamic; it seems to glide, using graceful, controlled movements with each step and turn. The transition from slow to quick motion is seamless, conducted without any jerky, awkward movements.

Now imagine a lion in the Serengeti, stalking its prey, using the same gliding movement as a domestic cat, but this time with a far more deadly purpose: survival. Imagine the moment has come for the lion to explode onto its prey for the final kill. It now stops, and performs a range of static stretches. I can't envisage this lion surviving for long in the wild!

For years athletes, footballers, netballers etc, and general keep fit enthusiasts believed that prior to any form of exercise, performing a range of static stretches was required to prevent injury and prepare the body for action. In professional sport, managers, coaches and trainers developed and perfected their own types of pre-training and pre-game routines, which invariably included lots of static stretching. Sports scientists and so-called 'fitness experts' have written about and designed programmes in books, magazines and newspapers advising on the benefits of static stretching immediately prior to physical activity.

Rather than being based on well-argued, scientific and medical research, such beliefs and advice have often been founded on myth, not fact or anecdotal evidence.

The facts

Very little research has been conducted into the effects of static stretching before physical exercise. (R. D. Herbert and M. Gabriel, BMJ, 2002).

Research that has been undertaken indicates that static stretching prior to physical exercise can have a detrimental effect on performance (R. D. Herbert and M. Gabriel, BMJ, 2002).

> "Stretching before and after exercising has no effect on delayed muscle soreness". (R. P. Pope, 1999).

> "Stretching before exercising does not produce a meaningful reduction in the risk of injury". (R. P. Pope, 1999).

Furthermore, it has been suggested (Oberg, 1993) that static stretching can reduce the eccentric strength of muscles, which is so vital for all dynamic activities.

David A. Lally, Ph.D., an exercise physiologist at the University of Hawaii-Manoa, completed a careful study of over 1,500 individuals who competed in a local marathon. His investigations linked pre-workout static stretching with a high risk of injury (Anderson, 2003).

Olympic Gold Medal Winner and World Champion Triple Jumper Jonathan Edwards, in a recent interview with *The Times* newspaper, indicated that he had changed his warm-up a number of years ago, from one incorporating a series of static movements to one where he works through a range of movements. As a consequence, he reported that he was able to maintain full muscle output during performance. Like many others, Edwards had discovered that static stretching reduces muscle power output for up to an hour, by as much as 20% (J. Edwards, *The Times*, Aug. 2002).

There has been anecdotal evidence for many years, from weight lifters, gymnasts and American footballers, that they failed to reach normal performance targets, height, speed, and lifted weight during training and competing after static stretches. If the muscle is made weaker, and its output reduced due to static stretching, then this will most likely lead to poor performance. A warm-up should prepare athletes to begin activities powerfully. It should prepare their bodies to perform the full range of movements demanded by their sport, without fear of tearing a muscle.

How do you pull a muscle? While moving. How then can you warm a muscle up when standing still?

However, a few years ago I recall working with a squad of elite rugby players including several internationals. Their warm-up comprised: a couple of laps of the pitch, to elevate the heart rate and to warm the body up; then players were paired off to perform buddy PNF (Proprioceptive Neuro-Muscular Facilitation) on each other on the ground; they then finished off with some short sharp sprints. It was hard to accept that this was considered a satisfactory pre-training warm-up, for these reasons: after the initial jog, the players would stop for over ten minutes to perform stretches on each other, in freezing conditions and at times lying on frozen ground. As already mentioned, PNF would weaken the players' output, thus making them more likely to injure themselves. Also, having elite athletes perform skills and drill sessions while underpowered would affect the quality of the training session. To go from stretching and cooling down to higher-intensity training invited soft tissue injuries such as sprains, strains and pulled muscles. These were a common occurrence, but were somehow accepted as an inevitable part of being a professional sportsperson.

Recently, I worked with a Premiership football team whose management introduced my system for achieving the aims of a dynamic flexibility warm-up, Dynamic Flex. They immediately reported a reduced incidence of soft tissue injuries and a marked improvement in overall team fitness and performance.

I get phone calls, letters and emails on a regular basis from all levels of sport and physical education, from professional strength-conditioners, personal trainers and teachers telling me how much difference the Dynamic Flex Warm-Up has made to their performance and preparation. Many of them also recount the old days when they used static stretching and the problems this type of warm-up caused. I remind them of the famous saying, "if you do what you've always done, you'll get what you've always gotten".

Children, schools and the education system

"One of the most disturbing assumptions is that the Dynamic Flex Warm-Up is for the elite athlete and not for school children."

The Dynamic Flex Warm-Up is not only ideal for children, but is also an essential part of their physical development. It is when we are in our youth that our bodies learn and remember the essentials of correct movement. The physiological development of young children requires them to move and perform during growth periods as the body is designed to. Young and alert nervous systems are hungry to learn and store in the muscle memory all these wonderful types of movements. A young person's neuromuscular system does not need much turning on.

The range of movements in a Dynamic Flex Warm-Up is crucial for the proper physical development of the individual. These patterns of movement become programmed into muscles' 'movement memory' like a tattoo. Think about the person who hasn't ridden a bike for twenty years, hops on one and within seconds has remastered the balance and co-ordination needed. Dynamic Flex Warm-Up can be introduced to children in a very simple structured form with only a few foundation exercises required. Gradually, these drills can be increased and made more complex, thus keeping a child interested and at the same time challenged. It is important to introduce and master one change at a time, and not bombard children with too much information in a short period of time. By introducing one new drill every week, over 10 weeks a full range of movement essentials can be worked on. Results will be tremendous.

Static stretching and the pseudo-science that recommends it is unfortunately a major part of the Curriculum for Physical Education in many parts of the world. This is in spite of the fact that in all cases great care must be taken when working with children. It stands to reason that any work with young people should not have a detrimental impact and should be well researched and founded. That our school curriculum could have embraced static stretching with its lack of research and obvious weaknesses is a serious concern for many. Students even have to include static stretching as the preferred manner in warming up when answering exam questions, for example.

If static stretching were so important as a system for warming up prior to activity, then surely at the end of classes prior to the morning, lunch and afternoon breaks, 10 minutes should be allocated for the children to perform their stretches so that they don't injure themselves in the playground. That this is not the case speaks volumes. On a personal basis, I can remember playing, jumping, dancing, skipping, running and dodging at school at all times of day without ever causing myself injury – and I had never heard of or performed static stretching.

I have actively questioned highly qualified individuals at many educational conferences, asking them to justify the inclusion of static stretching as part of warming up in the curriculum. They have no answers, satisfactory or otherwise. Some sit on the fence and take an impartial view. Others have written books in which the advice includes static stretching as a major part of the warming up process. These books are sold to schools and given to teachers in physical education departments as recommended resources. There has even been an attempt to confuse the education establishment by linking Dynamic Flex with ballistic stretching, when clearly they are very different. Undoubtedly, there is a large amount of evidence that highlights the potential problems of ballistic stretching. However, these problems do not apply when Dynamic Flex is carried out correctly. It has been inaccurately claimed that dynamic flexibility can trigger the stretch reflex and lead to muscle damage and soreness. In fact, Dynamic Flex is performed slowly enough that the stretch reflex mechanism of muscle contraction is not set off.

Through lobbying Government and delivering practical accessible training to primary and secondary teachers in the UK and Australia, I am delighted to say that changes in establishment thinking are being brought about. The Dynamic Flex Warm-Up is increasingly a vital element of training programmes and physical education in schools.

Currently over 70% of children do not participate in sport once they have left school (Chief Medical Officer, 2003). A health survey in England in 1998 reported that the scale of inactivity in children was alarmingly high: between the ages of two and five years, 52% of girls and 48% of boys are inactive; between the ages of six and 15 years, 65% of girls and 42% of boys are inactive. Dynamic Flex is not only an effective method of preparing children for activity, but it also provides the vital competencies of balance, co-ordination and rhythmic movement. Once these skills have been learned, increases in self-esteem and confidence follow, therefore making it more likely that children will remain involved in sport and physical activity.

Note: a special Dynamic Flex Warm-Up for children is on page 49.

Dynamic Flexibility Aims

A proper warm-up should:

- increase body temperature, specifically core (deep) muscle temperature;
- increase heart rate and blood flow;
- increase elasticity of muscular tissues;
- activate neuromuscular system;
- increase mental alertness; and
- rehearse the broad range of movements you will perform later.

How to use this book

A whole range of Dynamic Flex Warm-Up exercises suitable for all ages, fitness levels, active pastimes and sports is provided in Chapter 4. Each drill is given an intensity level, which is further explained in Chapter 1. The Suitability Table in Chapter 2 lists many popular sports and activities, from walking and dancing to tennis and American football. Sets and reps are also shown in all drills for adults, intermediates and beginners, as well as for ages 12 to 16 and 12 and under.

Simply refer to Chapter 1 and decide how intense you wish your exercise to be, according to your age, level of fitness and choice of sport. This will enable you to choose the correct drill for your own individual needs by matching your chosen level with the intensity level given at the foot of each drill page.

Then go to Chapter 2 and find your preferred sport in the Suitability Table. These are numbered from 1 to 3, and corresponding numbers are given under 'Suitability' at the foot of each drill page. This will help you decide which drills best fulfil the requirements of your own choice of sport or pastime.

Chapter 5 provides samples of complete sessions, ideal for all level of participants. You can also develop your own sessions by taking into account suitability and intensity levels. Remember: start small and simple, then gradually develop progressions.

Drills are often performed in grids, variations of which are given in Chapter 3. Needless to say, varying your drill routine by using different grids will help to stimulate and motivate you on a regular basis, without risk of boredom.

Also included is a special kids' Dynamic Flex Warm-Up.

Movement mechanics

Several drills within the book refer to the use of correct arm mechanics, lift mechanics and ground-to-foot contact. These are terms used in the development of proper running and movement techniques.

ARM MECHANICS

- Elbows held at 90°.
- Hands relaxed.
- The inside of the wrist should brush against your hips.
- The hand should move from the buttock cheek to the chest.
- Re-assert the arm drive as soon as possible after passing the ball or coming up from a lowered body position.

LIFT MECHANICS AND GROUND-TO-FOOT CONTACT

- 45° knee lift.
- Foot contacts the floor with the ball of the foot first.
- Front of the foot in a linear position.
- Foot-to-floor contact makes a tapping noise, not a thud or a slap.
- If the foot or the knee splays in or out, this means that power will not be transferred correctly.
- Keep off the heels.
- On the lift, the foot will transfer from pointing slightly downwards to pointing slightly upwards.

Each Dynamic Flex drill has been given an intensity level, which indicates that when the drill is performed properly you should reach a certain level of intensity. This is indicated in the guide below. The guide provides five levels of intensity; these are shown at the bottom of the page of each Dynamic Flex drill.

1. LOW INTENSITY   Ideal for all ages and fitness levels.

2. LOW TO MEDIUM   Ideal for all ages and fitness levels. Take care if you are returning after an injury.

3. MEDIUM INTENSITY   Ideal for the slightly fitter person.

4. MEDIUM TO HIGH   These exercises are designed to get you going. Ideal for all sports and fitness programmes. A person with a poor fitness level should build up to these drills.

5. HIGH   These drills will really get you firing on all cylinders. Ideal for serious trainers, athletes, sportsmen and sportswomen.

The table provides an important guide to a whole range of sports and activities that will benefit from a Dynamic Flex Warm-Up. The list includes low-activity sports such as lawn bowls to high-activity sports such as netball and football. Activities that cater for all age groups, from under 12s to senior citizens, will also greatly benefit.

Activity	Suitability rating	Activity	Suitability rating
American football	3	Jogging	1
Athletics	3	Judo	3
Australian rules football	3	Lacrosse	3
Badminton	3	Lawn bowls	1
Baseball	3	Martial arts	3
Basketball	3	Netball	3
Boxing	3	Orienteering	2/3
Cricket	3	PE, children under 10	2
Croquet	1	PE, children under 14	3
Cross-country skiing	3	PE, children over 14	3
Cycling	1	Play games	2
Dancing	2	Rugby	3
Driving	1	Skating	3
Fencing	2/3	Skiing	3
Football	3	Softball	2
Gaelic football	3	Sprinting	2
Gardening	1	Squash	3
Golf	2	Swimming	1
Handball	3	Table tennis	2
Hockey	3	Tennis	3
Hurdling	3	Ten-pin bowling	1
Ice hockey	3	Triathlon	2
Ice skating	3	Volleyball	3
Interval work	2	Walking	1

CHAPTER 3 GRID VARIATIONS

GRID | STANDARD SMALL SPACE GRID

Aim
To dynamically warm up in a small area.

Area/equipment
Indoor or outdoor restricted space and marker dots.

Description
Standard 10 m grid split up into two starting and finishing lines. Ideal for organising small squads and groups of children.

GRID SIDESTEP BACK GRID

Aim
To stimulate and motivate the warm-up with a variety of movement patterns. Ideal for squads and groups of children.

Area/equipment
Mark out an indoor or outdoor grid 20 m in length with markers placed at 2 m intervals. The width of the grid is variable depending on the size of the group. Place a line of markers on each side of the grid about 2 m away, with 1 m between each marker.

Description
Perform Dynamic Flex drills down the grid with the group splitting around the end markers to return on the outside of the grid. On reaching the markers, zigzag back through them.

Variations/progressions
- Replace the markers on the outside of the grid with Fast Foot ladder or hurdles.
- For a children's grid, shorten grid to 10 m in length.

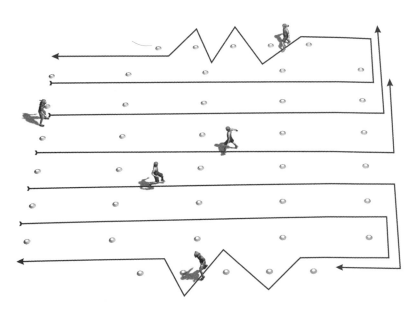

GRID SPLIT GRID

Aim

To integrate Dynamic Flex with sports-specific equipment to improve eye, hand and foot co-ordination, ball control and passing skills.

Area/equipment

Mark out an indoor or outdoor grid 10 m in length with an additional 5 m on the end (use different coloured markers). The width of the grid is variable depending on the size of the group or squad. Place a ball at the end of each channel for each person who will have just completed his/her Dynamic Flex drill.

Description

Perform Dynamic Flex drills down the grid over the first 10 m. On reaching the additional 5 m area, perform bean bag or ball skills up and back over it i.e. catching and juggling (manipulation skills). On completing the skills, pass the bean bag or ball to the next person, who will have just completed his/her Dynamic Flex drill.

Variations/progressions

Vary the manipulation skills and the objects passed to each other.

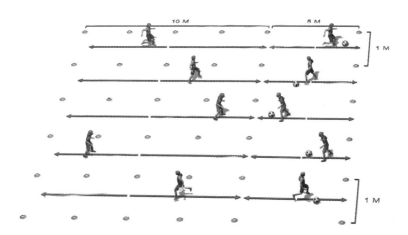

GRID   *ZIGZAG GRID*

Aim
To stimulate and motivate the warm-up and improve and challenge Dynamic Flex movements while moving and changing direction.

Area/equipment
Mark out an indoor or outdoor grid with markers 1 m apart forming a channel. Every 2 m along the grid, the markers move over a metre. The grid should be 10 m long with five changes of angle.

Description
Perform Dynamic Flex drills down the channel following the zigzag pattern.

Variations/progressions
Increase the length of grid to 20 m with 10 changes of angles.

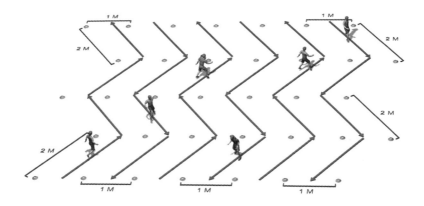

GRID   *CONTINUOUS WARM-UP*

Aim
To warm up with Dynamic Flex moving continuously. Ideal for open space, pre-jogging warm-up.

Area/equipment
Indoor or outdoor area.

Description
Perform set of drills moving in the same direction continuously until completed. Perform drills backwards and sideways.

Variations/progressions
Drills can be performed continuously up and back in a confined space.

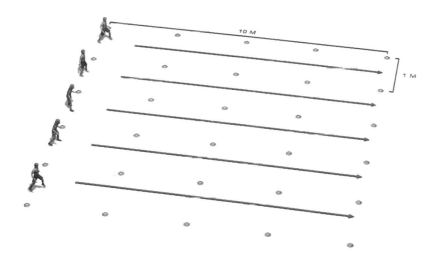

Additional Grid Variations

Aim
To warm up with Dynamic Flex using various grids to help motivate and stimulate.

Area/equipment
Indoor or outdoor space, various marker dots.

GRID | *THE CROSS*

Description
Place five marker dots in a cross formation with 5 m from centre to outside marker. Start drill at centre marker, perform drill forwards to outer marker, then backwards to centre marker. Repeat the drill clockwise or anti-clockwise, working out to the other markers.

Variations/progressions
Increase size of grid from 5 m to 10 m.

GRID | *W-GRID*

Description
Mark out a W formation using five marker dots, with the outer points 5 m apart and the centre points 2 m apart. Perform drill forwards and backwards following the W formation.

Variations/progressions
Increase the size of the W formation.

GRID | *STANDARD OUT AND BACK GRID*

Description
Set up a 20 m x 10 m grid marked out by marker dots placed at 1 m intervals for the channels, and 2 m intervals for the length. Perform drills in the channels between the marker dots up and down the grid.

Variations/progressions
Vary the size of the grid.

GRID · CIRCLE GRID

Description

Mark out a grid with an outer circle of markers 15 m in diameter and a centre circle of markers 5 m in diameter. Perform drills around the outside of the circle forwards and backwards. Then, for certain drills such as the Hamstring Walk, move inwards and outwards to and from the centre circle.

Variations/progressions

- Introduce manipulation skills.
- Increase size of circles depending on size of squad/group.

GRID · STAR GRID

Description

Use marker dots to mark out an eight-point star measuring 5 m from the outside point to the inner cicle. Perform drill from the outside point of the star to the inside point, then work from the insdie point to the outside.

Variations/progressions

Introduce manipulation skills.

GRID · ON-THE-SPOT DYNAMIC FLEX

Description

Mark out a grid with marker dots 2 m apart. Drills are performed on the spot within the space provided.

Variations/progressions

Additional movements can be introduced after each drill, so people move to a different spot.

GRID · THE SQUARE

Description

Mark out a square using marker dots 5 m apart. Perform a set of drills in the same direction around the square.

Variations/progressions

Occasionally perform drill diagonally across the square from corner to corner.

CHAPTER 4 THE DRILLS

DRILL *WALKING ON THE BALLS OF THE FEET*

Aim
To improve shin stretch, ankle mobility, balance and co-ordination. To increase body temperature.

Description
Cover the length of the grid by walking on the balls of the feet. Return to the start by repeating the drill backwards.

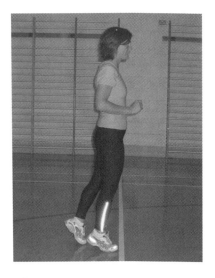

Key Teaching Points
■ Do not walk on the ends of the toes.

■ Keep off the heels.

■ Maintain correct arm mechanics (refer to page x).

■ Maintain an upright posture.

Sets and Reps
Adult:	1 × 20 m forwards
	1 × 20 m backwards
Intermediate/beginner:	1 × 10–15 m forwards
	1 × 10–15 m backwards
	(depending on fitness level)
12–16 years:	1 × 15 m forwards
	1 × 15 m backwards
12 and under:	1 × 8 m forwards
	1 × 8 m backwards

Variations/Progressions
■ Perform the drill laterally but do not allow the feet to come together completely. Push off with the back foot, do not pull with the lead foot.

■ Perform the drill forwards for 3 steps, sideways for 3 steps, backwards for 3 steps, then sideways, leading with opposite shoulder, for 3 steps, continuously up and down the grid.

Suitability
1, 2, 3

Intensity
Low

DRILL ANKLE FLICK

Aim

To stretch calf and improve ankle mobility, balance, co-ordination and rhythm of movement. To prepare for good foot-to-floor contact. To increase body temperature.

Description

Cover the length of the grid in a skipping manner where the ball of the foot plants then flicks up towards the shin; move as if bouncing. Return to the start by repeating the drill backwards.

Key Teaching Points

■ Work off the ball of the foot, not the toes.

■ Practise the first few steps on the spot before moving off.

■ Maintain correct arm mechanics (refer to page x).

■ Maintain an upright posture.

Sets and Reps

Adult:	1 × 20 m forwards
	1 × 20 m backwards
Intermediate/beginner:	1 × 10–15 m forwards
	1 × 10–15 m backwards
	(depending on fitness level)
12–16 years:	1 × 15 m forwards
	1 × 15 m backwards
12 and under:	1 × 8 m forwards
	1 × 8 m backwards

Variations/Progressions

Perform the drill laterally.

Suitability

1, 2, 3

Intensity

Low

DRILL *SMALL SKIP*

Aim

To improve lower leg flexibility, ankle mobility, balance, co-ordination and rhythm, and to develop positive foot-to-ground contact. To increase body temperature.

Description

Cover the length of the grid in a low skipping manner. Return to the start by repeating the drill backwards.

Key Teaching Points

- Knee to be raised to about a 45–55° angle.

- Work off the ball of the foot.

- Maintain correct arm mechanics (refer to page x).

- Maintain an upright posture.

- Maintain a good rhythm.

Sets and Reps

Adult:	1 × 20 m forwards
	1 × 20 m backwards
Intermediate/beginner:	1 × 10–15 m forwards
	1 × 10–15 m backwards
	(depending on fitness level)
12–16 years:	1 × 15 m forwards
	1 × 15 m backwards
12 and under:	1 × 8 m forwards
	1 × 8 m backwards

Variations/Progressions

Perform the drill laterally.

Suitability

1, 2, 3

Intensity

Low to medium

DRILL LOW KNEE-OUT SKIP

Aim

To stretch inner thigh and improve hip mobility. To develop an angled knee drive, balance, co-ordination and rhythm. To increase body temperature.

Description

Cover the length of the grid in a skipping motion. The knee moves from the centre of the body to a position outside the body but below the waistline before returning to the central position. Return to the start by repeating the drill backwards.

Key Teaching Points

- Feet start in line and move outwards as the knee is raised.
- Work off the balls of the feet.
- The knee is to be pushed out and back, not rolled out.
- Maintain correct arm mechanics (refer to page x).
- The movement should be smooth, not jerky.
- Knee should not be raised above waistline.

Sets and Reps

Adult:	1 × 20 m forwards
	1 × 20 m backwards
Intermediate/beginner:	1 × 10–15 m forwards
	1 × 10–15 m backwards
	(depending on fitness level)
12–16 years:	1 × 15 m forwards
	1 × 15 m backwards
12 and under:	1 × 8 m forwards
	1 × 8 m backwards

Variations/Progressions

Perform the drill laterally.

Suitability

1, 2, 3

Intensity

Low

DRILL *LOW KNEE-ACROSS SKIP*

Aim
To improve outer hip flexibility and hip mobility over a period of time. To develop balance and co-ordination. To increase body temperature.

Description
Cover the length of the grid in a skipping motion, where the knee comes across the body but below the waistline. Return to the start by repeating the drill backwards.

Key Teaching Points
- Do not force an increased range of motion (ROM).
- Work off the balls of the feet.
- Maintain a strong core.
- Maintain an upright posture.
- Control the head by looking forward at all times.
- Use the arms primarily for balance.

Sets and Reps
Adult:	1 × 20 m forwards
	1 × 20 m backwards
Intermediate/beginner:	1 × 10–15 m forwards
	1 × 10–15 m backwards
	(depending on fitness level)
12–16 years:	1 × 15 m forwards
	1 × 15 m backwards
12 and under:	1 × 8 m forwards
	1 × 8 m backwards

Variations/Progressions
Perform the drill laterally.

Suitability
1, 2, 3

Intensity
Low

DRILL *SINGLE KNEE DEAD-LEG LIFT*

Aim

To improve buttock flexibility and hip mobility. To isolate the correct 'running cycle' motion for each leg.

Description

Cover the length of the grid by bringing the knee of one leg quickly up to a 90° position. The other leg should remain as straight as possible with a very short lift away from the ground throughout the movement. Ratio should be 1 lift to every 4 steps. Work one leg on the way down the grid and the other on the return.

Key Teaching Points

- Do not walk – take the knee above the 90° angle.

- Strike the floor with the ball of the foot.

- Keep the foot pointing forward.

- Maintain correct movement mechanics (refer to page x).

Sets and Reps

Adult:	1 × 20 m forwards
	1 × 20 m backwards
Intermediate/beginner:	1 × 10–15 m forwards
	1 × 10–15 m backwards
	(depending on fitness level)
12–16 years:	1 × 15 m forwards
	1 × 15 m backwards
12 and under:	1 × 8 m forwards
	1 × 8 m backwards

Variations/Progressions

Vary the lift ratio, e.g. 1 lift to every 2 steps.

Suitability

1, 2, 3

Intensity

Medium to high

Aim

To develop economic knee drive, stretch the side of the quadriceps and prepare for an efficient lateral running technique. To increase body temperature.

Description

Cover the length of the grid with the left or right shoulder leading, taking short lateral steps. Return with the opposite shoulder leading.

Key Teaching Points

- Keep the hips square.
- Work off the balls of the feet.
- Do not skip.
- Do not let the feet cross over.
- Maintain an upright posture.
- Do not sink into the hips or lean over.
- Do not overstride – use short sharp steps.
- Maintain correct arm mechanics (refer to page x).

Sets and Reps

Adult:	1 × 20 m left shoulder leading
	1 × 20 m right shoulder leading
Intermediate/beginner:	1 × 10–15 m left shoulder leading
	1 × 10–15 m right shoulder leading
	(depending on fitness level)
12–16 years:	1 × 15 m left shoulder leading
	1 × 15 m right shoulder leading
12 and under:	1 × 8 m left shoulder leading
	1 × 8 m right shoulder leading

Variations/Progressions

- Practise lateral angled zig-zag runs.
- Turn every 3 or 4 steps.

Suitability

1, 2, 3

Intensity

Low to medium

DRILL PRE-TURN

Aim
To prepare the hips for a turning action without committing the whole body. To increase
body temperature and improve body control.

Description
Cover the length of the grid by performing a
lateral movement. The heel of the back foot is
moved to a position almost alongside the lead
foot. Just before the feet come together, the
lead foot is moved away laterally. Return to the
start by repeating the drill but lead with the
opposite shoulder. The heel of the back foot is
raised no more than 6–8 inches. The knee
should not be raised above waistline level.

Key Teaching Points
- The back foot must not cross the lead foot.
- Work off the balls of the feet.
- Maintain correct arm mechanics (refer to page x).
- Maintain an upright posture.
- Do not sink into the hips or fold at the waist.
- Do not use a high knee lift; the angle should be no more than 45°.

Sets and Reps
Adult:	1 × 20 m left shoulder leading
	1 × 20 m right shoulder leading
Intermediate/beginner:	1 × 10–15 m left shoulder leading
	1 × 10–15 m right shoulder leading
	(depending on fitness level)
12–16 years:	1 × 15 m left shoulder leading
	1 × 15 m right shoulder leading
12 and under:	1 × 8 m left shoulder leading
	1 × 8 m right shoulder leading

Variations/Progressions
Turn and repeat drill on opposite leg, the maintaining the same direction.

Suitability
1, 2, 3

Intensity
Low to medium

DRILL CARIOCA

Aim

To improve hip mobility and speed, which will increase the firing of nerve impulses over a period of time. To develop balance and co-ordination while moving and twisting. To increase body temperature.

Description

Cover the length of the grid by moving laterally. The rear foot crosses in front of the body and then moves around to the back of the body. Simultaneously, the lead foot will do the opposite. The arms also move across the front and back of the body.

Key Teaching Points

- Start slowly and build up the tempo.
- Work off the balls of the feet.
- Keep the shoulders square.
- Do not force the ROM.
- Use the arms primarily for balance.

Sets and Reps

Adult:	1 × 20 m left shoulder leading
	1 × 20 m right shoulder leading
Intermediate/beginner:	1 × 10–15 m left shoulder leading
	1 × 10–15 m right shoulder leading
	(depending on fitness level)
12–16 years:	1 × 15 m left shoulder leading
	1 × 15 m right shoulder leading
12 and under:	1 × 8 m left shoulder leading
	1 × 8 m right shoulder leading

Variations/Progressions

- Perform the drill laterally with a partner (mirror drills), i.e. one initiates/leads the movement while the other attempts to follow.
- Change direction of leading shoulder every 4 to 5 metres.

Suitability

1, 2, 3

Intensity

Medium

University of South Wales

Tel: 01443 668666

Borrowed Items 18/12/2013 15:56
XXXX2178

Item Title	Due Date
Changing kids' games	10/01/2014
RFU guide for coaches : fitness and conditioning	10/01/2014
Dynamic flexibility	10/01/2014
Rugby : steps to success	10/01/2014
Anatomy and human movement : structure and function	10/01/2014

Amount Outstanding: £1.80

Thankyou for using this unit
Thank you
Diolch yn fawr

DRILL *SKIPPIOCA*

Aim
To improve hip and ankle mobility, balance, co-ordination and rhythm. To increase body temperature.

Description
Cover the length of the grid by skipping with the feet remaining shoulder-width apart and knees facing outwards at all times. Return to the start by repeating the drill backwards.

Key Teaching Points
- Keep off the heels.
- Maintain correct arm mechanics (refer to page x).
- Maintain an upright posture.
- Do not take the thigh above a 90° angle.

Sets and Reps

Adult:	1 × 20 m forwards
	1 × 20 m backwards
Intermediate/beginner:	1 × 10–15 m forwards
	1 × 10–15 m backwards
	(depending on fitness level)
12–16 years:	1 × 15 m forwards
	1 × 15 m backwards
12 and under:	1 × 8 m forwards
	1 × 8 m backwards

Variations/Progressions
Perform the drill laterally

Suitability
2, 3

Intensity
Medium to high

DRILL HIGH KNEE-LIFT SKIP

Aim
To improve buttock flexibility and hip mobility. To increase ROM over a period of time. To develop rhythm. To increase body temperature.

Description
Cover the length of the grid in a high skipping motion. Return to the start by repeating the drill backwards.

Key Teaching Points
 Thigh to be taken past the 90° angle.
- Work off the balls of the feet.
- Maintain a strong core.
- Maintain an upright posture.
- Control the head by looking forward at all times.
- Maintain correct arm mechanics (refer to page x).

Sets and Reps
Adult:	1 × 20 m forwards
	1 × 20 m backwards
Intermediate/beginner:	1 × 10–15 m forwards
	1 × 10–15 m backwards
	(depending on fitness level)
12–16 years:	1 × 15 m forwards
	1 × 15 m backwards
12 and under:	1 × 8 m forwards
	1 × 8 m backwards

Variations/Progressions
Perform the drill laterally.

Suitability
3

Intensity
High

DRILL   *HIGH KNEE-OUT SKIP*

Aim

To increase the range of movement of the hip and stretch the inner thigh. To develop a higher angled knee drive, greater balance and co-ordination. To increase body temperature.

Description

Cover the length of the grid in a skipping motion. The knee moves from the centre of the body to a position outside the body above the waist before returning to the central position. Return to the start by repeating the drill skipping backwards.

Key Teaching Points

■ Feet start in line and move outwards as the knee is raised.

■ Work off the balls of the feet.

■ The knee is to be pushed out and back, not rolled out.

■ Maintain correct arm mechanics (refer to page x).

■ The movement should be smooth, not jerky.

■ Knee to be raised above the waistline if possible.

Sets and Reps

Adult:	1 × 20 m forwards
	1 × 20 m backwards
Intermediate/beginner:	1 × 10–15 m forwards
	1 × 10–15 m backwards
	(depending on fitness level)
12–16 years:	1 × 15 m forwards
	1 × 15 m backwards
12 and under:	1 × 8 m forwards
	1 × 8 m backwards

Variations/Progressions

■ Perform the drill laterally.

■ Alternate knee lift: 2 to right, 2 to left.

Suitability

2, 3

Intensity

High

DRILL HIGH KNEE-ACROSS SKIP

Aim
To increase outer hip flexibility and hip mobility over a period of time. To develop greater balance and co-ordination. To increase body temperature.

Description
Cover the length of the grid in a skipping motion where the knee comes across the body, with the knee being raised outside and above the waistline. Return to the start by repeating the drill backwards.

Key Teaching Points
- Do not force an increased ROM.
- Work off the balls of the feet.
- Maintain a strong core.
- Maintain an upright posture.
- Control the head by looking forward at all times.
- Use the arms primarily for balance.
- Knee to be raised above and outside the waistline if possible.

Sets and Reps
Adult:	1 × 20 m forwards
	1 × 20 m backwards
Intermediate/beginner:	1 × 10–15 m forwards
	1 × 10–15 m backwards
	(depending on fitness level)
12–16 years:	1 × 15 m forwards
	1 × 15 m backwards
12 and under:	1 × 8 m forwards
	1 × 8 m backwards

Variations/Progressions
- Perform the drill laterally.
- Alternate knee lift: 2 to right, 2 to left.

Suitability
2, 3

Intensity
High

DRILL *WIDE SKIP*

Aim

To improve hip and ankle mobility. To improve balance, co-ordination and rhythm. To increase body temperature.

Description

Cover the length of the grid by skipping. The feet should remain wider than shoulder-width apart and the knees should face outwards at all times. Return to the start by repeating the drill backwards.

Key Teaching Points

- Keep off the heels.
- Maintain correct arm mechanics (refer to page x).
- Maintain an upright posture.
- Do not take the thigh above a 90° angle.

Sets and Reps

Adult:	1 × 20 m forwards
	1 × 20 m backwards
Intermediate/beginner:	1 × 10–15 m forwards
	1 × 10–15 m backwards
	(depending on fitness level)
12–16 years:	1 × 15 m forwards
	1 × 15 m backwards
12 and under:	1 × 8 m forwards
	1 × 8 m backwards

Variations/Progressions

Perform the drill laterally.

Suitability

1,2,3

Intensity

Medium to high

DRILL INNER HAMSTRING FLICK

Aim
To improve front inner thigh stretch and hip mobility. To increase body temperature.

Description
Cover the length of the grid by moving forwards, alternating leg flicks, where the heel moves up to the front inside of the opposite thigh near the groin. Repeat the drill backwards after completing the first section of the grid.

Key Teaching Points
- Work off the balls of the feet.
- Develop a rhythm.
- Maintain an upright posture.
- Do not sink into the hips.
- Start slowly and build up the tempo.
- Use a good arm drive.

Set and Reps

Adult:	1 × 20 m forwards
	1 × 20 m backwards
Intermediate/beginner:	1 × 10–15 m forwards
	1 × 10–15 m backwards
	(depending on fitness level)
12–16 years:	1 × 15 m forwards
	1 × 15 m backwards
12 and under:	1 × 8 m forwards
	1 × 8 m backwards

Variations/Progressions
Perform the drill laterally.

Suitability
2, 3

Intensity
Medium to high

DRILL OUTER HAMSTRING FLICK

Aim
To improve front, back and side thigh stretch and hip mobility. To increase body temperature.

Description
Cover the length of the grid by moving forwards, alternating leg flicks, where the heel moves up to the outside of the top of the thigh and hip. Repeat the drill backwards after completing the first section of the grid.

Key Teaching Points
- Work off the balls of the feet.
- Develop a rhythm.
- Maintain an upright posture.
- Do not sink into the hips.
- Start slowly and build up the tempo.
- Use a good arm drive.

Set and Reps

Adult:	1 × 20 m forwards
	1 × 20 m backwards
Intermediate/beginner:	1 × 10–15 m forwards
	1 × 10–15 m backwards
	(depending on fitness level)
12–16 years:	1 × 15 m forwards
	1 × 15 m backwards
12 and under:	1 × 8 m forwards
	1 × 8 m backwards

Variations/Progressions
Perform the drill laterally.

Suitability
2, 3

Intensity
Medium to high

Learning Resources
Centre

DRILL HAMSTRING BUTTOCK FLICK

Aim
To stretch front and back of thigh and improve hip mobility. To increase body temperature.

Description
Cover the length of the grid by moving forwards alternating leg flicks, where the heel moves up towards the buttocks. Return to the start repeating the drill backwards.

Key Teaching Points
- Start slowly and build up the tempo.
- Work off the balls of the feet.
- Maintain an upright posture.
- Do not sink into the hips.
- Try to develop a rhythm.

Sets and Reps
Adult:	1 × 20 m forwards
	1 × 20 m backwards
Intermediate/beginner:	1 × 10–15 m forwards
	1 × 10–15 m backwards
	(depending on fitness level)
12–16 years:	1 × 15 m forwards
	1 × 15 m backwards
12 and under:	1 × 8 m forwards
	1 × 8 m backwards

Variations/Progressions
- Perform the drill laterally.
- Perform the drill as above, but flick the heel to the outside of the buttocks.

Suitability
2, 3

Intensity
Medium to high

| DRILL | *RUSSIAN WALK* |

Aim

To stretch back of thigh and improve hip mobility and ankle stabilisation. To develop balance and co-ordination and increase body temperature.

Description

Cover the length of the grid by performing a walking march with a high, extended step. Imagine that the aim is to scrape the sole of your shoe down the front of a door. Return to the start by repeating the drill backwards.

Key Teaching Points

■ Lift the knee before extending the leg.

■ Work off the balls of the feet.

■ Try to keep off the heels, particularly on the back foot.

■ Keep the hips square.

Sets and Reps

Adult:	1 × 20 m left shoulder leading
	1 × 20 m right shoulder leading
Intermediate/beginner:	1 × 10–15 m left shoulder leading
	1 × 10–15 m right shoulder leading
	(depending on fitness level)
12–16 years:	1 × 15 m left shoulder leading
	1 × 15 m right shoulder leading
12 and under:	1 × 8 m left shoulder leading
	1 × 8 m right shoulder leading

Variations/Progressions

■ Perform the drill backwards.

■ Perform the drill moving sideways.

Suitability

1, 2, 3

Intensity

Low

DRILL WALKING HAMSTRING

Aim
To stretch back of thigh.

Description
Cover the length of the grid by extending the lead leg forward, placing the whole of the foot on the ground and pushing the hips slowly backwards as far as comfortably possible, without sinking into the hips, keeping the spine upright at all times. Walk forwards and repeat on the opposite leg; continue in this manner alternating the lead leg.

Key Teaching Points
- Keep the spine in a straight line.
- Do not bend over.
- Control the head by looking forward at all times.
- Work at a steady pace, do not rush.

Sets and Reps
Adult:	1 × 20 m left shoulder leading
	1 × 20 m right shoulder leading
Intermediate/beginner:	1 × 10–15 m left shoulder leading
	1 × 10–15 m right shoulder leading
	(depending on fitness level)
12–16 years:	1 × 15 m left shoulder leading
	1 × 15 m right shoulder leading
12 and under:	1 × 8 m left shoulder leading
	1 × 8 m right shoulder leading

Variations/Progressions
When hips have extended back as far as possible, roll the foot up onto the heel until you can feel the calf stretching, then repeat on the other leg.

Suitability
1, 2, 3

Intensity
Low

DRILL *KNEE TO CHEST*

Aim
To stretch the gluteals and improve linear hip mobility. To increase body temperature.

Description
Stand tall and raise the knee of one leg up to the chest; to lightly increase the stretch, squeeze the knee in by placing the hands around the front of the knee and applying pressure. Repeat the drill on the other leg.

Key Teaching Points
- Work off the ball of the foot on the straight leg.
- Apply pressure steadily.
- Stay tall and look ahead.

Sets and Reps
Adult:	1 × 20 m forwards
	1 × 20 m backwards
Intermediate/beginner:	1 × 10–15 m forwards
	1 × 10–15 m backwards
	(depending on fitness level)
12–16 years:	1 × 15 m forwards
	1 × 15 m backwards
12 and under:	1 × 8 m forwards
	1 × 8 m backwards

Variations/Progressions
- On releasing the leg, use a knee out skip.
- Perform drill laterally.

Suitability
1, 2, 3

Intensity
Low

DRILL *WALKING LUNGE*

Aim

To stretch front of hip and thigh. To develop balance and co-ordination, and increase body temperature.

Description

Cover the length of the grid by performing a walking lunge. The front leg should be bent with a 90° angle at the knee and the thigh in a horizontal position. The back leg should also be at a 90° angle but with the knee touching the ground and the thigh in a vertical position. Return to the start by repeating the drill backwards.

Key Teaching Points

- Try to keep the hips square.
- Maintain a strong core and keep upright.
- Maintain good control.
- Persevere with backward lunges – these are difficult to master.

Sets and Reps

Adult:	1 × 20 m forwards
	1 × 20 m backwards
Intermediate/beginner:	1 × 10–15 m forwards
	1 × 10–15 m backwards
	(depending on fitness level)
12–16 years:	1 × 15 m forwards
	1 × 15 m backwards
12 and under:	1 × 8 m forwards
	1 × 8 m backwards

Variations/Progressions

- Perform the drill with handweights.
- Perform the drill while catching and passing a ball in the down position.

Suitability

1, 2, 3

Intensity

Low to medium

DRILL SIDE LUNGE

Aim
To stretch inner thigh and gluteal muscles. To develop balance and co-ordination. To increase body temperature.

Description
Cover the length of the grid by performing lateral lunges. Take a wide sideways step and simultaneously lower the gluteals towards the ground. Return to the start with the opposite shoulder leading.

Key Teaching Points
- Do not bend at the waist or lean forwards.
- Try to keep off the heels.
- Maintain a strong core and keep upright.
- Use the arms primarily for balance.

Sets and Reps
Adult:	1 × 20 m left shoulder leading
	1 × 20 m right shoulder leading
Intermediate/beginner:	1 × 10–15 m left shoulder leading
	1 × 10–15 m right shoulder leading
	(depending on fitness level)
12–16 years:	1 × 15 m left shoulder leading
	1 × 15 m right shoulder leading
12 and under:	1 × 8 m left shoulder leading
	1 × 8 m right shoulder leading

Variations/Progressions
- Work in pairs facing each other and chest-passing the ball.
- Perform the drill changing from left to right shoulder after each sideways lunge, in a rotating fashion.

Suitability
2, 3

Intensity
Low to medium

DRILL ANGLED LUNGE

Aim
To stretch front of hip and thigh and to develop balance and co-ordination at different angles. To increase body temperature.

Description
Cover the length of the grid by performing a walking angled lunge. The front leg should be moved out at a 45° angle to the other leg. The back leg should be bent at a 90° angle but with the knee touching the ground and the thigh in a vertical position. Return to the start by repeating the drill backwards.

Key Teaching Points
- Try to keep the hips square.
- Maintain a strong core and keep upright.
- Maintain good control
- Persevere with backward lunges – they are difficult to master.

Sets and Reps
Adult:	1 × 20 m left leg leading
	1 × 20 m right leg leading
Intermediate/beginner:	1 × 10–15 m left leg leading
	1 × 10–15 m right leg leading
	(depending on fitness level)
12–16 years:	1 × 15 m left leg leading
	1 × 15 m right leg leading
12 and under:	1 × 8 m left leg leading
	1 × 8 m right leg leading

Variations/Progressions
- Perform the drill with handweights.
- Perform the drill while catching and passing a ball in the down position.

Suitability
1, 2, 3

Intensity
Low to medium

DRILL   ADVANCED CORE LUNGE

Aim

To improve front of hip and thigh stretch and develop core strength, balance and co-ordination. To increase body temperature.

Description

Cover the length of the grid, performing a walking lunge with arm raises. The front leg should be bent with a 90° angle at the knee and the thigh in a horizontal position. The back leg should also be at a 90° angle with the knee touching the ground and the thigh in a vertical position. On the way down, the arms are pushed out and raised above the head as the back knee touches the ground. This is repeated for the other leg.

Key Teaching Points

- Try to keep the hips square.
- Maintain a strong core and keep upright.
- Maintain good control.
- Look forward at all times.
- Use a smooth arm action.

Sets and Reps

Adult:	1 × 20 m forwards; 1 × 20 m backwards
Intermediate/beginner:	1 × 10–15 m forwards; 1 × 10–15 m backwards (depending on fitness level)
12–16 years:	1 × 15 m forwards; 1 × 15 m backwards
12 and under:	1 × 8 m forwards; 1 × 8 m backwards

Variations/Progressions

- Push arms out and back.
- Draw a figure of eight with arms held out.
- Move the arms from side to side.
- Perform single arm punches out in front and above.

Suitabllity

2, 3

Intensity

Medium

DRILL HURDLE WALK

Aim
To stretch inner and outer thigh and increase ROM. To develop balance and co-ordination and increase body temperature.

Description
Cover the length of the grid by walking in a straight line and alternating the lifting leg as if going over a high hurdle. Return to the start repeating the drill backwards.

Key Teaching Points
- Try to keep the body square as the hips rotate.
- Work off the balls of the feet.
- Maintain an upright posture.
- Do not sink into the hips or bend over at the waist.
- Imagine that you are actually stepping over a barrier.

Sets and Reps
Adult:	1 × 20 m forwards
	1 × 20 m backwards
Intermediate/beginner:	1 × 10–15 m forwards
	1 × 10–15 m backwards
	(depending on fitness level)
12–16 years:	1 × 15 m forwards
	1 × 15 m backwards
12 and under:	1 × 8 m forwards
	1 × 8 m backwards

Variations/Progressions
Alternate the lifting leg after completing 3 hurdles.

Suitability
1, 2, 3

Intensity
Low to medium

Aim
To prepare the hips for a higher, more dynamic turning action without committing the whole body. To increase body temperature and improve body control.

Area/Equipment
An indoor or outdoor grid 20 m in length. The width of the grid is variable depending on the size of the squad.

Description
Cover the length of the grid by performing a lateral movement. The heel of the back foot is moved to a position almost alongside the lead foot. Just before the feet come together, the lead foot is moved away laterally. Return to the start by repeating the drill leading with the opposite shoulder. The heel of the back foot is raised so that it is in line with or higher than the opposite knee. The knee will therefore be raised above waist level.

Key Teaching Points
- The back foot must not cross the lead foot.
- Work off the balls of the feet.
- Maintain correct arm mechanics (refer to page x).
- Maintain an upright posture.
- Do not sink into the hips or fold at the waist.
- If possible, raise knee above the waist.

Sets and Reps
Adult:	1 × 20 m left shoulder leading
	1 × 20 m right shoulder leading
Intermediate/beginner:	1 × 10–15 m left shoulder leading
	1 × 10–15 m right shoulder leading
	(depending on fitness level)
12–16 years:	1 × 15 m left shoulder leading
	1 × 15 m right shoulder leading
12 and under:	1 × 8 m left shoulder leading
	1 × 8 m right shoulder leading

Variations/Progressions N/A

Suitability 2, 3

Intensity Medium to high

DRILL SKIP AND SHOULDER ROLL

Aim
To develop good foot-to-ground contact, shoulder warmth, balance and co-ordination. To increase body temperature.

Description
Cover the length of the grid with a short, quick skipping motion, rotating the arms and shoulders forwards while skipping forwards, and rotating the arms and shoulders backwards while skipping backwards.

Key Teaching Points
- Work off the balls of the feet.
- Maintain an upright posture.
- Use a large range of motion with the arms and shoulders.

Sets and Reps
Adult:	1 × 20 m forwards
	1 × 20 m backwards
Intermediate/beginner:	1 × 10–15 m forwards
	1 × 10–15 m backwards
	(depending on fitness level)
12–16 years:	1 × 15 m forwards
	1 × 15 m backwards
12 and under:	1 × 8 m forwards
	1 × 8 m backwards

Variations/Progressions
Perform drill laterally.

Suitability
1, 2, 3

Intensity
Medium

DRILL *JOG, HUG AND TWIST*

Aim
Core, shoulder and arm stretch.

Description
Place left hand outside right shoulder with the
left arm across the chest. Place right hand on
the outside of the left shoulder at the same
time. Imagine you are giving yourself a bear
hug. Jog, hug and rotate from left to right of
the waist. Repeat backwards.

Key Teaching Points
- Keep an upright posture.
- Develop a rhythm while rotating at the
  waist.
- Keep the pressure of the squeeze the same
  throughout the drill.

Sets and Reps
Adult:	1 × 20 m forwards
	1 × 20 m backwards
Intermediate/beginner:	1 × 10–15 m forwards
	1 × 10–15 m backwards
	(depending on fitness level)
12–16 years:	1 × 15 m forwards
	1 × 15 m backwards
12 and under:	1 × 8 m forwards
	1 × 8 m backwards

Variations/Progressions
Perform drill laterally.

Suitability
1, 2, 3

Intensity
Low to medium

DRILL SPOTTY DOGS

Aim

To improve shoulder and arm mobility, activate core muscles, improve balance and co-ordination and increase body temperature.

Description

Cover length of grid by simultaneously chopping the legs and arms, left leg to right arm, then right leg to left arm. The arm should move from the side of the body up to the side of the face.

Key Teaching Points

- Keep off the heels.
- Arm action is a chop, not a punch.
- Land and take off on the balls of the feet.
- Maintain upright posture.
- Keep the head up.

Sets and Reps

Adult:	1 × 20 m forwards
	1 × 20 m backwards
Intermediate/beginner:	1 × 10–15 m forwards
	1 × 10–15 m backwards
	(depending on fitness level)
12–16 years:	1 × 15 m forwards
	1 × 15 m backwards
12 and under:	1 × 8 m forwards
	1 × 8 m backwards

Variations/Progressions

Perform the drill laterally.

Suitability

1, 2, 3

Intensity

Medium to high

DRILL CROSS-STEP AND PUNCH

Aim
To develop outside hip mobility, foot-to-ground contact, chest and shoulder warmth, co-ordination, balance and rhythm of movement. To increase body temperature.

Description
Rotate the body so that the right foot lands at the front and the left foot rotates to the back, while at the same time punching out with the right arm. Skip forwards, so that the left foot comes to the front and the right foot rotates to the back with the left arm punching forwards.

Key Teaching Points
- Work off the balls of the feet.
- Keep off heels and toes.
- Maintain an upright posture.
- Develop rhythm with the skip and punch.

Sets and Reps
Adult:	1 × 20 m forwards
	1 × 20 m backwards
Intermediate/beginner:	1 × 10–15 m forwards
	1 × 10–15 m backwards
	(depending on fitness level)
12–16 years:	1 × 15 m forwards
	1 × 15 m backwards
12 and under:	1 × 8 m forwards
	1 × 8 m backwards

Variations/Progressions
Perform drill laterally.

Suitability
2, 3

Intensity
Medium to high

DRILL TWIST AGAIN

Aim
To improve rotational hip mobility and speed. To develop balance, foot control and co-ordination and increase body temperature.

Description
Stand tall with feet together and jump forwards, moving the feet to the left and then across the body to the right. The arms should be fired across the body for balance and speed.

Key Teaching Points
■ Try to develop a rhythm.

■ Work off the balls of the feet.

■ Maintain an upright posture and look ahead.

■ Do not sink into the hips or bend over at the waist.

■ Imagine that you are actually stepping over a barrier.

Sets and Reps
Adult:	1 × 20 m forwards
	1 × 20 m backwards
Intermediate/beginner:	1 × 10–15 m forwards
	1 × 10–15 m backwards
	(depending on fitness level)
12–16 years:	1 × 15 m forwards
	1 × 15 m backwards
12 and under:	1 × 8 m forwards
	1 × 8 m backwards

Variations/Progressions
Perform the drill sideways changing from left to right shoulders.

Suitability
1, 2, 3

Intensity
Medium to high

DRILL ICE SKATING

Aim
To increase ankle mobility, lateral foot control, balance and co-ordination. To increase body temperature.

Description
Lean slightly forward and swing the arms across the body while side-stepping from left to right as an ice skater would.

Key Teaching Points
- Keep the head up.
- Do not sink into the hips or lean over.
- Try to land on the balls of the feet.

Sets and Reps

Adult:	1 × 20 m left shoulder leading
	1 × 20 m right shoulder leading
Intermediate/beginner:	1 × 10–15 m left shoulder leading
	1 × 10–15 m right shoulder leading
	(depending on fitness level)
12–16 years:	1 × 15 m left shoulder leading
	1 × 15 m right shoulder leading
12 and under:	1 × 8 m left shoulder leading
	1 × 8 m right shoulder leading

Variations/Progressions
Alternate from short to long step.

Suitability
2, 3

Intensity
Medium to high

Aim

To increase the ROM in the hip region. To increase body temperature.

Description

Face and lean against a wall or fence at about a 20–30° angle. Swing the leg across the body from one side to the other. Repeat with the other leg.

Key Teaching Points

- Do not force an increased ROM.
- Work off the ball of the support foot.
- Lean with both hands against the wall/ fence.
- Keep the hips square.
- Do not look down.
- Gradually speed up the movement.

Sets and Reps

Adult:	7–10 on each leg
Intermediate/beginner:	4–7 on each leg
	(depending on fitness level)
12–16 years:	6–7 on each leg
12 and under:	4–5 on each leg

Variations/Progressions

Lean against a partner.

Suitability

1, 2, 3

Intensity

Low

DRILL WALL DRILL – LINEAR LEG FORWARD AND BACK

Aim
To increase the ROM in the hip region. To increase body temperature.

Description
Stand beside a wall or fence, using the nearer arm to hold on to it for balance. Take the outer leg back and swing it forward in a straight line. Repeat with the other leg

Key Teaching Points
- Do not force an increased ROM.
- Work off the ball of the support foot.
- Lean with both hands against the wall/fence.
- Do not look down.
- Gradually speed up the movement.

Sets and Reps
Adult:	7–10 on each leg
Intermediate/beginner:	4–7 on each leg
	(depending on fitness level)
12–16 years:	6 -7 on each leg
12 and under:	4–5 on each leg

Variations/Progressions
Lean against a partner.

Suitability
1, 2, 3

Intensity
Low

DRILL WALL DRILL – KNEE ACROSS BODY

Aim
To increase the ROM in the hip region. To increase body temperature.

Description
Face and lean against a wall or fence at about a 20–30° angle. From a standing position, drive one knee upwards and across the body. Repeat with the other leg.

Key Teaching Points
- Do not force an increased ROM.
- Work off the ball of the support foot.
- Lean with both hands against the wall/fence.
- Keep the hips square.
- Do not look down.
- Gradually speed up the movement.
- Imagine you are trying to get your knee up and across your body to the opposite hip.

Sets and Reps
Adult:	7–10 on each leg
Intermediate/beginner:	4–7 on each leg
	(depending on fitness level)
12–16 years:	6–7 on each leg
12 and under:	4–5 on each leg

Variations/Progressions
Lean against a partner.

Suitability
1, 2, 3

Intensity
Low

DRILL WALL DRILL – SCORPION

Aim
To increase the ROM in the hip, hamstring and lower back region. To improve balance and co-ordination and increase body temperature.

Description
Stand beside a wall or fence, using the nearer arm to hold it for balance. Bend at the waist, keeping the head up and the spine in a straight line; simultaneously raise the outer leg behind you, bending the knee, trying to touch the back of your buttocks with your heel. The outer arm should be held out to help balance. Repeat on the other side.

Key Teaching Points
- Do not force an increased ROM.
- Work off the ball of the support foot.
- Keep the hips level.
- Do not look down.
- Perform drill slowly and develop a rhythm.

Sets and Reps
Adult:	7–10 on each leg
Intermediate/beginner:	4–7 on each leg (depending on fitness level)
12–16 years:	6–7 on each leg
12 and under:	4–5 on each leg

Variations/Progressions
Lean against a partner.

Suitability
1, 2, 3

Intensity
Low

DRILL WALL DRILL – HIP THRUST

Aim
To increase the ROM in the hip region and to stretch the thigh, calf and lower back with a resultant increase in body temperature.

Description
Face and lean against a wall or fence at about a 20–30° angle. From a standing position, keeping the spine straight, bend the knees to about 45°. Then thrust upwards, bringing the hips up towards the wall and finishing on the balls of the feet.

Key Teaching Points
- Keep the spine in a straight line.
- Do not sink into the hips.
- Bend at the knees, not at the waist.
- Try to develop a rhythm.
- Do not look down.

Sets and Reps
Adult:	7–10 thrusts
Intermediate/beginner:	4–7 thrusts (depending on fitness level)
12–16 years:	6–7 thrusts
12 and under:	4–5 thrusts

Variations/Progressions
Lean against a partner.

Suitability
1, 2, 3

Intensity
Low

DRILL | *PAIR DRILL – LATERAL PAIR RUNS*

Aim
To develop running skills in a more game-specific situation. To stimulate balance and co-ordination and to practise reassertion of the correct mechanics. To increase body temperature.

Description
Refer to Lateral Running drill (page 16). The players face each other 2–3 feet apart and cover the length of the grid. Occasionally, they can push each other.

Key Teaching Points
■ Refer to Lateral Running drill (see page 16).

■ When off balance or after being pushed, the focus should be on the reassertion of the correct arm and foot mechanics.

Sets and Reps
Adult:	1 × 20 m left leg leading
	1 × 20 m right leg leading
Intermediate/beginner:	1 × 10–15 m left leg leading
	1 × 10–15 m right leg leading
	(depending on fitness level)
12–16 years:	1 × 15 m left leg leading
	1 × 15 m right leg leading
12 and under:	1 × 8 m left leg leading
	1 × 8 m right leg leading

Variations/Progressions
Introduce a ball and pass hand-to-hand and then hand-to-foot.

Suitability
3

Intensity
Medium to high

DRILL PAIR DRILL – JOCKEYING

Aim
To stimulate defensive and attacking close-quarter movement patterns. To increase body temperature.

Description
Stand facing each other and cover the grid, working both forwards and backwards. The player moving forwards (attacker) will show their left and then their right shoulder alternately in a rhythmic motion. The player moving backwards (defender) covers the attacking player's movements by mirroring them.

Key Teaching Points
- Take short steps.
- Do not cross the feet.
- Maintain a strong core and an upright posture.
- Do not sink into the hips.
- Keep your eyes on the opponent at all times.

Sets and Reps
Adult:	1 × 20 m left leg leading
	1 × 20 m right leg leading
Intermediate/beginner:	1 × 10–15 m left leg leading
	1 × 10–15 m right leg leading
	(depending on fitness level)
12–16 years:	1 × 15 m left leg leading
	1 × 15 m right leg leading
12 and under:	1 × 8 m left leg leading
	1 × 8 m right leg leading

Variations/Progressions
Introduce a ball to the attacking player who presses forward with the ball at his or her feet, transferring it from left to right to keep the defender on his or her toes.

Suitability
3

Intensity
Medium to high

Dynamic Flex Warm–Up for children

When working with children, it is important to keep it simple. Do not overwhelm them with too many drills at once – introduce new drills one or two at a time, weekly or fortnightly. You many find that it is beneficial to practise the drills first on the spot and to initially work at a slow pace so that the children can improve performance before adding intensity.

The following session is called the '2 on, 2 off'. Each drill is performed twice, the first time to practise and get it right and the second time to perfect the exercise.

Drill	Suitability	Intensity
Walking on the Balls of the Feet	1, 2, 3	Low
Ankle Flick	1, 2, 3	Low
Walking on the Balls of the Feet	1, 2, 3	Low
Ankle Flick	1, 2, 3	Low
Small Skip	1, 2, 3	Low/medium
Low Knee-Out Skip	1, 2, 3	Low
Small Skip	1, 2, 3	Low/medium
Low Knee-Out Skip	1, 2, 3	Low
Low Knee-Across Skip	1, 2, 3	Low
Single Knee Dead-Leg Lift	1, 2, 3	Medium/high
Low Knee-Across Skip	1, 2, 3	Low
Single Knee Dead-Leg Lift	1, 2, 3	Medium/high
Lateral Running	1, 2, 3	Low/medium
Carioca	1, 2, 3	Medium
Lateral Running	1, 2, 3	Low/medium
Carioca	1, 2, 3	Medium
Hamstring Buttock Flick	2, 3	Medium/high
Russian Walk	1, 2, 3	Low
Hamstring Buttock Flick	2, 3	Medium/high
Russian Walk	1, 2, 3	Low
Walking Hamstring	1, 2, 3	Low
Spotty Dogs	1, 2, 3	Medium/high
Walking Hamstring	1, 2, 3	Low
Spotty Dogs	1, 2, 3	Medium/high

Dynamic Flex Warm–Up for low activity pastimes and sports

The following Dynamic Flex session is ideal for those involved in low activity pastimes with an average fitness level.

Drill	Suitability	Intensity
Walking on the Balls of the Feet	1, 2, 3	Low
Ankle Flick	1, 2, 3	Low
Small Skip	1, 2, 3	Low/medium
Low Knee-Out Skip	1, 2, 3	Low
Low Knee-Across Skip	1, 2, 3	Low
Single Knee Dead-Leg Lift	1, 2, 3	Medium/high
Lateral Running	1, 2, 3	Low/medium
Pre-Turn	1, 2, 3	Low/medium
Carioca	1, 2, 3	Medium
Wide Skip	1, 2, 3	Medium/high
Russian Walk	1, 2, 3	Low
Walking Hamstring	1, 2, 3	Low
Hurdle Walk	1, 2, 3	Low/medium
Walking Lunge	1, 2, 3	Low/medium
Skip and Shoulder Roll	1, 2, 3	Medium
Jog, Hug and Twist	1, 2, 3	Low/medium
Wall Drill – Leg Out and Across the Body	1, 2, 3	Low
Wall Drill – Linear Leg Forward and Back	1, 2, 3	Low
Wall Drill – Knee Across Body	1, 2, 3	Low
Twist Again	1, 2, 3	Medium/high

Dynamic Flex Warm–Up for fitness enthusiasts

The following session is ideal for warming up prior to squash, tennis, running and sports and pastimes that are generally played by the keep-fit and sports enthusiast.

Drill	Suitability	Intensity
Walking on the Balls of the Feet	1, 2, 3	Low
Ankle Flick	1, 2, 3	Low
Small Skip	1, 2, 3	Low/medium
Low Knee-Out Skip	1, 2, 3	Low
Low Knee-Across Skip	1, 2, 3	Low
Single Knee Dead-Leg Lift	1, 2, 3	Medium/high
Lateral Running	1, 2, 3	Low/medium
Pre-Turn	1, 2, 3	Low/medium
Carioca	1, 2, 3	Medium
High Knee-Lift Skip	3	High
High Knee-Out Skip	2, 3	High
High Knee-Across Skip	2, 3	High
Outer Hamstring Flick	2, 3	Medium/high
Russian Walk	1, 2, 3	Low
Walking Hamstring	1, 2, 3	Low
Walking Lunge	1, 2, 3	Low/medium
Hurdle Walk	1, 2, 3	Low/medium
Skip and Shoulder Roll	1, 2, 3	Medium
Cross-Step and Punch	2, 3	Medium/high
Wall Drill – Leg Out and Across the Body	1, 2, 3	Low
Wall Drill – Linear Leg Forward and Back	1, 2, 3	Low
Wall Drill – Knee Across Body	1, 2, 3	Low
Spotty Dogs	1, 2, 3	Medium/high

Dynamic Flex Warm–Up for high intensity amateur and professional sports

The following session is ideal for the more serious fitness and sport enthusiast, as well as professionals involved in high-intensity fitness and sport performance. Ideal for football, rugby, hockey, netball, boxing etc.

Drill	Suitability	Intensity
Small Skip	1, 2, 3	Low/medium
Skip and Shoulder Roll	1, 2, 3	Medium
Ankle Flick	1, 2, 3	Low
Low Knee-Out Skip	1, 2, 3	Low
Low Knee-Across Skip	1, 2, 3	Low
Single Knee Dead-Leg Lift	1, 2, 3	Medium/high
Lateral Running	1, 2, 3	Low/medium
Pre-Turn	1, 2, 3	Low/medium
Carioca	1, 2, 3	Medium
Skippioca	2, 3	Medium/high
High Knee-Lift Skip	3	High
High Knee-Out Skip	2, 3	High
High Knee-Across Skip	2, 3	High
Wide Skip	1, 2, 3	Medium/high
Inner Hamstring Flick	2, 3	Medium/high
Outer Hamstring Flick	2, 3	Medium/high
Hamstring Buttock Flick	2, 3	Medium/high
Russian Walk	1, 2, 3	Low
Walking Hamstring	1, 2, 3	Low
Angled Lunge	1, 2, 3	Low/medium
Hurdle Walk	1, 2, 3	Low/medium
Advanced Core Lunge	2, 3	Medium
High Pre-Turn	2, 3	Medium/high
Wall Drill – Leg Out and Across the Body	1, 2, 3	Low
Wall Drill – Linear Leg Forward and Back	1, 2, 3	Low
Wall Drill – Knee Across Body	1, 2, 3	Low
Wall Drill – Scorpion	1, 2, 3	Low
Wall Drill – Hip Thrust	1, 2, 3	Low
Ice Skating	2, 3	Medium/high
Twist Again	1, 2, 3	Medium/high

References

Bennett, S. (1999)· 'New Muscle Research Findings', Muscle Symposium, AIS, Canberra, Australia

Gleim, G. W. and McHugh, M. P. (1997), 'Flexibility and Its Effects on Sports Injury and Performance', *Sports Medicine*, 24(5): 289–99

Herbert, R.D. and Gabriel, M. (2002), 'Effects of stretching before or after exercising on muscle soreness and risk of injury: a systematic review', *The British Medical Journal*, 325:468–470

Kokkonen, J., Nelson A.G. and Cornwell, A., (1998), 'Acute muscle stretching inhibits maximal strength performance', *Research Quarterly for Exercise and Sport*, Vol 4, pp. 411–15

Oberg, B. (1993), 'Evaluation and improvement of strength in competitive athletes', Harms-Ringdahl, K. (ed), *Muscle Strength*, pp 167–185, Churchill Livingstone, Edinburgh

Pope, R. C. (1999), 'Skip the Warm-up', *New Scientist*, 18 Dec 164(2214):23

Index of drills

Learning Resources
Centre